Meteorology
Cool Women Who Weather Storms

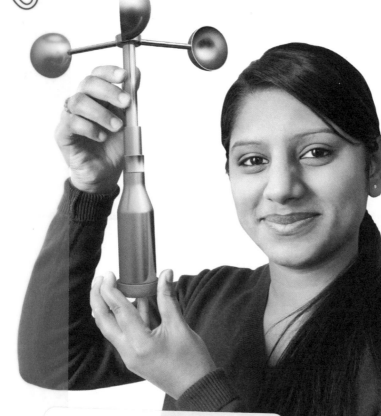

Karen Bush Gibson

Illustrated by
Lena Chandhok

Nomad Press
A division of Nomad Communications
10 9 8 7 6 5 4 3 2 1

This book was manufactured by CGB Printers,
North Mankato, Minnesota, United States
August 2017, Job #228801

ISBN Softcover: 978-1-61930-541-0
ISBN Hardcover: 978-1-61930-537-3

Educational Consultant, Marla Conn
Thank you to the American Meteorological Society.

Questions regarding the ordering of this book should be addressed to
Nomad Press
2456 Christian St.
White River Junction, VT 05001
www.nomadpress.net

Printed in the United States.

~ Titles in the Girls in Science Series ~

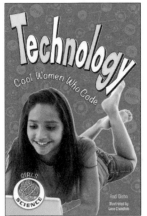

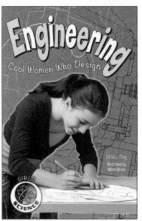

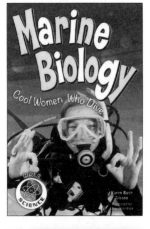

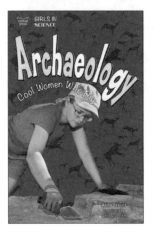

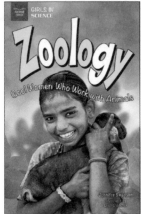

Check out more titles at www.nomadpress.net

How to Use This Book

In this book you'll find a few different ways to explore the topic of women in meteorology.

The essential questions in each Ask & Answer box encourage you to think further. You probably won't find the answers to these questions in the text, and sometimes there are no right or wrong answers! Instead, these questions are here to help you think more deeply about what you're reading and how the material connects to your own life.

There's a lot of new vocabulary in this book! Can you figure out a word's meaning from the paragraph? Look in the glossary in the back of the book to find the definitions of words you don't know.

Are you interested in what women have to say about meteorology? You'll find quotes from women who are professionals in the meteorology field. You can learn a lot by listening to people who have worked hard to succeed!

Primary sources come from people who were eyewitnesses to events. They might write about the event, take pictures, or record the event for radio or video. Why are primary sources important?

Interested in primary sources? Look for this icon.

PS

Use a QR code reader app on your tablet or other device to find online primary sources. You can find a list of URLs on the Resources page. If the QR code doesn't work, try searching the Internet with the Keyword Prompts to find other helpful sources.

CONTENTS

atmosphere climate global warming meteorologist weather forecast climatology satellite data predict cyclical phenomena altitude radar evolution humidity equator barometer ozone precipitation stratosphere hurricane supercell topography circulation dissertation astronomy radiosonde almanac air mass FEMA cell front analyze convection monsoon condensation matter remote sensing tropical wave natural disaster vapor observatory mentor STEM theory pattern scud rotation dimension pressure density frequency crops export lake-effect snow origin recruit diversity velocity physics current variability de-ice

INTRODUCTION

What Is Meteorology?

What are you going to wear tomorrow? Will soccer practice be canceled because of rain? Is it going to be hot enough to go swimming? Maybe you'll have a day off from school because of the snow! Our entire lives are affected by the weather. It can be a perfect day to have a cookout or storms can make it dangerous to step out the door. The people who study meteorology help us stay safe and help us understand what is happening above our heads.

66 Nature is so powerful, so strong. Capturing its essence is not easy—your work becomes a dance with light and the weather. It takes you to a place within yourself. 99

—Annie Leibovitz,
photographer

Meteorology is the study of the atmosphere and everything that happens there, including the weather. The word *meteorology* comes from the Greek word *meteoron*, which translates to "something that happens high in the sky."

IMPORTANCE OF METEOROLOGY

Meteorology affects day-to-day life. It impacts how we dress, our travel plans, and business. From the earliest beginnings of human history, weather has played an important role. For example, humans realized that weather has a lot to do with the outcome of crops. Seamen learned to read the skies and adjust sailing routes and schedules based upon weather. Good weather meant abundant crops and easy travel. Bad weather resulted in limited food supplies and the destruction of ships.

Countries that exported goods across oceans soon learned the importance of trade winds. When ships traveled with a strong trade wind, it traveled faster and reached its destination sooner. Against these winds, shipping took longer and cost more money.

Some of the most dramatic photographs are because of weather

photo credit: NOAA/Department of Commerce, Ralph F. Kresge

Weather also affects humans through natural disasters, which can be devastating. Floods, tornadoes, and hurricanes are just some of the weather phenomena that can claim lives and wipe out communities. That's why the weather forecasts of meteorology are so important.

Accurate weather forecasts can save lives, but it's not the only type of meteorology. In recent years, meteorologists have begun working more closely with climatologists as knowledge about global warming has increased.

> **66** Climate is what we expect,
> weather is what we get. **99**
>
> **—Mark Twain,**
> writer

Most American Meteorological Society (AMS) members (96 percent) believe climate change is occurring. Global warming may impact the frequency or severity of extreme weather and events, such as hurricanes. Changes in precipitation patterns lead to flooding in some areas and drought in others.

Relationships between climate change and weather are being studied by the National Center for Atmospheric Research (NCAR) in Boulder, Colorado. NCAR studies the atmosphere and how it is being affected by global changes. Surface and ocean temperatures have increased. Polar ice has shrunk significantly. The earth's sea levels rose about 7 inches during the last century and are continuing to rise. These changes affect all life on Earth.

Although weather can be devastating, it is also fascinating to many people. Are you mesmerized by the power of a thunderstorm? Do you wonder how tornadoes form? Weather invites the questions what, where, when, how, and why. Meteorologists seek to answer those questions, and by doing so, help others.

In *Meteorology: Cool Women Who Weather Storms*, you'll read about three fascinating women who enjoy observing and investigating the atmosphere.

Weather and Climate

What is the difference between weather and climate? It's all related to time. Weather is the condition of the atmosphere during a short period of time. Is it sunny today? Will there be rain this week? Climate is how the atmosphere behaves during long periods of time. Climate is determined by several factors, including latitude, which is distance north or south of the equator, and local topography, such as mountains and other features of the land. Altitude, the height above the level of the sea, and distance to oceans also affect climate.

Climate is always changing. Throughout history, there have been and will continue to be natural changes in the climate due to things such as solar activity or volcanic eruptions. A major change in climate that lasts several decades is referred to as climate change. Scientists have discovered that the concentration of carbon dioxide in the atmosphere during the past 60 years has increased much faster than any other time during the past 800,000 years. This dramatic change is primarily caused by human activity, such as the use of fossil fuels and deforestation. It is these changes that have led to global warming.

You can read the National Aeronautics and Space Administration's (NASA's) Twitter account about its climate change studies and discoveries.

NASA climate Twitter 🔍

These women worked hard to get where they are today, and they love sharing their passion for meteorology with others. Broadcast meteorologist Kelly Cass has a particular interest in severe weather, such as tropical storms and snowstorms. After being recognized for blizzard reporting at a local station, she went on to work at the Weather Channel.

Working for the National Weather Service is something Bianca Hernandez has always wanted to do. She works in a weather forecast office studying daily climate data, such as temperature and precipitation, for her region.

Pamela Heinselman is a research meteorologist at the National Oceanic and Atmospheric Administration (NOAA) National Severe Storms Laboratory. In addition to analyzing radar data, she also teaches meteorology to college students.

The careers of these three women show us that there are many paths to meteorology. In this book, we'll learn more about what they do and why. But first, let's explore the fascinating world of meteorology that these women have chosen as their careers.

Ask & Answer

Why is meteorology an important career for women? What would science be like if only one race or gender worked in it?

CHAPTER 1

A History of Meteorology

Do you ever look at the sky and make weather predictions according to the clouds hovering above your house? Today, you can check many websites and find out the weather all around the world. On the television and radio, weather forecasters are standing by to offer updates on the developing weather. It's easy to learn what to expect for weather in the coming days.

WHAT HAPPENS IN THE CLOUDS?

The atmosphere is a layer of gases that surrounds a planet. The word *atmosphere* comes from a Greek word meaning "surrounding vapor." Earth's atmosphere is about 65 to 75 miles thick.

Meteorology studies the part of the atmosphere closest to the earth. This part is called the troposphere, and it's measured from the earth's surface to about 5 miles above the surface.

The word *troposphere* means "sphere of change." This is where most weather takes place. Sometimes weather also occurs in the next level of the atmosphere, called the stratosphere.

Meteorology is the science of weather. Meteorologists observe what's happening in the air, take measurements, and analyze data from a variety of sources. The basic tools used by meteorologists include barometers to measure air pressure, temperature gauges to measure air temperature, and hygrometers to measure humidity.

Most of today's data is gathered electronicly. It comes from radar, weather balloons, and planes that measure pressure, temperatures, and humidity. Weather satellites over the equator and the North and South Poles also provide meteorologists with data.

COMPONENTS OF WEATHER

Many types of weather are observed, tracked, and studied by meteorologists. For instance, precipitation comes down in various forms and intensities, depending on origin and location. There are actually 11 forms of precipitation. A few are rain, showers, thunderstorms, fog, drizzle, hail, sleet, and snow.

Temperature relates to location as well. The seasons and winds also play parts. Wind is actually air masses that move from high-pressure to low-pressure areas. Land- and sea-based air masses are volumes of air with consistent temperatures and humidity. Cells are air masses that can lead to storms—thunderstorms, snowstorms, tornadoes, and hurricanes.

The orange layer of the earth's atmosphere is the troposphere
photo credit: NASA

When we observe and study the weather, we look for patterns. Knowing these patterns helps meteorologists make predictions that help people.

Global patterns show heat, wind, and moisture moving from the tropics around the equator to the North and South Poles. Long-term patterns include events such as El Niño, which occurs only every few years. El Niño is a warming of the ocean surface off the western coast of South America that creates unusual weather patterns in different parts of the world. Long-term patterns disrupt the circulation of the atmosphere. Because of this, they cause dramatic changes to weather and ocean currents.

While we think of weather as local, or the events we can see out our windows, it's actually global. What happens on the other side of the world has an effect on the weather where you live. It's all connected!

The science of meteorology has been developing for thousands of years. It's natural for humans to look around for clues about weather events. It was only fairly recently, though, that we developed the tools we needed to make sense of all these clues.

EARLY METEOROLOGY

When ancient civilizations developed agriculture, understanding the weather became even more important. Why do you think this is true?

Thousands of years ago, Babylonian and Chinese astronomers tried to predict weather changes based upon astronomical events. The Greek philosopher Aristotle (384–322 BCE) studied meteorology. In 340 BCE, he wrote a four-volume work called *Meteorologica*, in which he shared his theories about weather phenomena.

Aristotle's work was based on ideas, however, and not on the scientific method. The scientific method is the way scientists ask questions and do experiments to try to prove their ideas.

Like the Babylonians and Chinese before them, many Mesoamerican civilizations, such as the Maya, saw a relationship between astronomy and the weather. They built observatories where they could observe the night sky. The Maya began to measure and record the different phenomena they witnessed.

Ask & Answer

Many early discoveries in meteorology were made by physicists. Physics is a branch of science that studies matter and energy. How is meteorology connected to other sciences?

Other people also recorded observations of the sky and of natural occurrences. The first known recorded account of a hurricane was written by explorer Christopher Columbus (c. 1451–1506). His fleet of ships was hit by a hurricane off the coast of present-day Dominican Republic and Haiti in 1502.

As more people recorded the weather they observed, more connections could be made between atmospheric conditions and the weather. And those connections led to the modern science of meteorology and weather forecasting.

EARLY TOOLS OF METEOROLOGY

The invention of meteorological instruments helped advance our knowledge about the weather. The first-known meteorological instrument was a hygrometer, which measures humidity. It was invented by Nicholas Cusa (1401–1464) in the mid-1400s.

Two hundred years later, Italian physicist Evangelista Torricelli (1608–1647) observed that when air pressure changed, so did the weather. He invented the barometer in 1643 to measure air pressure.

It was a German physicist who developed the most important meteorological instrument of the next century. His name was Daniel Fahrenheit (1686–1736). Can you guess what he invented?

66 The storm was terrible and on that night the ships were parted from me. Each one of them was reduced to an extremity, expecting nothing save death; each one of them was certain that the others were lost. 99

—Christopher Columbus,
on first encountering a hurricane

Although Galileo Galilei (1564–1642) had invented the first thermometer in 1592, Daniel Fahrenheit refined it by placing a glass tube closed at one end in mercury. He devised a scale so that when the mercury moved in the tube, people could record the temperature.

Another astronomer, Edmond Halley (1656–1742), is well-known for discovering the comet that bears his name. Edmond Halley also published the first meteorological chart and came up with an explanation of how trade winds develop from warm air at the equator.

America's Founding Fathers George Washington (1732–1799) and Thomas Jefferson (1743–1826) both recorded the weather in their journals. In fact, Jefferson recorded the temperature on July 4, 1776. At 1 p.m., it was 76 degrees Fahrenheit.

When Samuel Morse (1791–1872) invented the telegraph in the mid-nineteenth century, the science of meteorology made another leap. The telegraph allowed weather data to be shared almost instantaneously. Why was this important?

Meteorological offices were created around the globe to share information and create weather maps that incorporated large areas. Meteorologists analyzed the data and began making weather predictions.

In the 1920s, Norwegian scientists used physics to explain air masses and fronts. They discovered that large-scale cold and warm air masses moved and followed patterns. This explained many weather systems.

Also in the 1920s, the radiosonde was invented. The radiosonde is a small, lightweight box with weather instruments and a radio transmitter. These are carried into the atmosphere by weather balloons. Radiosondes can collect data up to an altitude of about 20 miles before the weather balloons burst.

By the 1950s, scientists began using computers to create weather predictions. They did this by entering data points and equations called algorithms. Scientists were able to make the first large-scale weather predictions and share them by radio and television.

WHERE WERE THE WOMEN?

We don't know much about early female meteorologists. We do know that a book titled *Cloud Crystals: A Snow-Flake Album Collected and Edited by a Lady* was published in 1864.

Check the Almanac

The *Old Farmer's Almanac* has been predicting the weather in the United States since George Washington was president! An annual calendar of dates and data, almanacs were used for gardening, advice, and weather predictions. It is still published annually and people still swear by it. You can find a long-range weather forecast for your region at this website. Why might a long-range forecast be useful?

Old Farmer's Almanac long range 🔍

The author/illustrator was a woman named Frances E. Knowlton Chickering. Little is known about her other than her keen observation skills. In her book, she drew different types of snowflakes and explained the atmospheric conditions that produced each.

Some early female meteorologists established weather observation stations throughout the world. In Italy, Caterina Scarpellini (1808–1873) founded the Meteorological Ozonometric Station in Rome. She recorded information about weather and ozone conditions in her region.

British scientist Eleanor Anne Ormerod (1828–1901) bought a microscope and began studying various insects while she was in her twenties. The Royal Horticultural Society awarded her a Silver Medal for her work, but her father disapproved of her working as a scientist.

After her father's death, Eleanor joined her brother at a weather observation station and took meteorological observations. She became interested in the relationships between meteorology and insects.

Sarah Frances Whiting

Sarah Frances Whiting (1847–1927) was a physicist, astronomer, and meteorologist. She was born in Wyoming, New York. Her father was a professor who oversaw her education and made sure she received instruction in mathematics and physics. Sarah became interested in physics as she helped her father prepare science demonstrations for his classes.

After Sarah graduated from Ingham University in 1865, she began teaching at a girls' school. Meanwhile, she kept learning by attending science lectures in physics and astronomy wherever she could. She studied laboratory physics at Massachusetts Institute of Technology (MIT), the first undergraduate physics laboratory in the United States.

Eleanor published her work and became the first female fellow of the Royal Meteorological Society. She later established her own meteorological station and continued publishing until her death.

Several women were charter members of the American Meteorological Society, formed in 1919. These included Grace Evangeline Davis (1870–1955) who studied physics and meteorology and later taught meteorology at Wellesley College.

In 1875, Sarah was recruited to teach physics at a new women's college, Wellesley College. Three years later, she opened the second undergraduate physics laboratory in the United States. She also made the first X-ray photographs in the country.

Sarah was the first woman invited to join the New England Meteorological Society. She created a course in meteorology and an observing station and her students collected data for the U.S. Weather Bureau. Sarah served as the director of the Whitin Observatory at Wellesley College from 1904 until her retirement in 1916.

66 A winter's storm, an open window, a bit of fur or velvet, and a common magnifier, will bring any curious inquirer upon his field of observation with all the necessary apparatus, and he has only to open his eyes to find the grand and beautiful laboratory of nature open to his inspection. 99

—Frances E. Knowlton Chickering

Gladys Wrigley (1885–1975) was another scientist who was a charter member of the American Meteorological Society. She was the first woman to earn a PhD in geography and an important scientific editor at the *Geographical Review*.

By writing about meteorology and establishing observation stations, these early pioneers in the field demonstrated that women are more than capable of being scientists. Each of these female scientists broke down barriers for the women who followed.

WAR-TIME METEOROLOGY

With the arrival of World War II, the military realized how much the weather impacted missions and battles. Large-scale research and experimentation led to the creation of new technologies—in particular, meteorological radar. Radar could detect airplanes and ships, but it could also detect the direction of wind and precipitation patterns.

Ask & Answer

Why do you think so little information is available on early female scientists?

Here's how radar works. An active sensor in a radar dish sends out radio waves. These bounce off particles in the atmosphere before returning to Earth. A computer processes the pulses and determines the dimensions of the precipitation, as well as the speed and direction the clouds and precipitation are moving. This allows scientists to track storms and warn people in their paths!

Before the United States entered World War II, the U.S. Weather Bureau had only two female employees. But during the war, many men at the weather bureau left to fight—or to forecast the weather—for the war.

Weather observation and forecasting became an area in which women were called upon to fill the void. In 1945, more than 900 women were hired as observers and forecasters. As in other professions, women showed they could do the job just as well, and sometimes better, than men.

Dorothy Taylor was one of those women. The 19-year-old worked at the weather observation station in Casper, Wyoming.

When a heavy snowstorm isolated the station on April 12, 1945, Dorothy worked through the storm without a break. Every six hours, she did all her observations and measurements, despite heavy snow, freezing temperatures, and strong winds.

When the war ended and men returned from the battlefields, some women lost their positions. Others continued working for the U.S. Weather Bureau, and later the National Weather Service.

UNDERSTANDING METEOROLOGY

One of the many fascinating things about the weather is how it's always changing. Meteorologists look at the weather from day to day and from region to region. Weather is energy, heat, and moisture. It can be influenced by space, ocean tides, and human activity. Meteorology begins with air circulation.

Cold air tends to be dense, so it sinks. Warm air is less dense, so it rises. This sinking and rising creates a circular current. The process of the circulation of air is called convection, and it's an important principle in meteorology. Energy, heat, and moisture are transferred during convection.

> 66 A weather forecast takes in our knowledge of history, our present understanding of science, our best guesses of the future. 99
>
> **—Lauren Redniss,**
> author of *Thunder & Lighting*

Global atmospheric circulation is a large movement of air that distributes heat across the world. George Hadley (1685–1768) was an amateur meteorologist who first described the theory of the trade winds. When warm air rises and pushes against cooler, denser air above, there is a loop. Called "Hadley cells," they determine the direction and strength of the trade winds. Hadley cells affect circulation around the globe. They create patterns of convection in tropical and equatorial areas.

Pressure, like convection, is another meteorological principle. Pressure is involved in large-scale weather systems such as hurricanes and winter storms.

Clouds

Clouds are an important weather indicator. Luke Howard (1772–1864), considered the father of modern meteorology, was the first to come up with a cloud classification system in the early nineteenth century. The World Meteorological Organization lists three levels of clouds, each with distinct temperatures, pressures, and density. Within these three levels, there are 10 basic cloud types, according to the National Weather Service. You can learn the names of these clouds and see examples at this website.

cloud types

A low-pressure area over Iceland

photo credit: NASA

Low-pressure systems occur when atmospheric pressure at the surface is less than in the surrounding environment. They circulate counter-clockwise. This forces air up, which leads to clouds, condensation, and precipitation.

High-pressure systems occur when atmospheric pressure at the surface is greater than in the surrounding environment. These systems circulate in a clockwise motion that result in a sinking motion in the atmosphere, leaving us with clear and sunny skies.

High-pressure systems containing wind and moisture seek out low-pressure systems. This movement of pressure systems causes a system to rotate in a counterclockwise direction if it occurs north of the equator, and in a clockwise direction if it forms south of the equator.

For example, when a low-pressure system develops over tropical waters in the Western Hemisphere, the system sucks up moisture from the tropical water. This leads to convection, increasing wind speed, and falling pressure.

Weather occurs on different scales of space and time. Those meteorological scales are microscale, mesoscale, synoptic scale, and global scale.

- Microscale focuses on brief phenomena in temperatures and small geographic areas, including processes between soil, vegetation, and surface water. The transfer of heat, gas, and liquid between these surfaces is measured. Phenomena may range in size from half an inch to a few miles.

- Mesoscale phenomena range in size from about a mile to 620 miles. This is an intermediate scale.

- Synoptic scale covers larger areas, up to thousands of miles in size. It's related to pressure systems. Most pressure systems change through time. Others are semi-permanent and are responsible for climate.

- Global scale measures weather patterns from the tropics to the North and South Poles. Hadley cells, such as the trade winds, are a part of this scale.

TODAY'S
METEOROLOGICAL TOOLS

Although weather stations sometimes use non-computerized tools, most of today's measurements are taken electronically.

The most critical measurements for forecasting are:

- Air pressure

- Air temperature

- Air humidity

- Air movement

Doppler radar is a popular tool. It is used by meteorologists to help create their weather forecasts. This type of radar sends out electromagnetic wave fields that are reflected back by things in the air, such as precipitation. Doppler radar provides data that helps scientists understand how weather patterns, such as thunderstorms, grow and fade in strength.

66 The weather is the backdrop
for every moment in our lives.
It can brighten, or darken, the mood.
The weather never fails to fascinate,
captivate, and pique my curiosity. **99**

—Jen Carfagno,
on-camera meteorologist, The Weather Channel

Ocean, Meet Atmosphere

The earth's rotation affects the direction of winds and the ocean currents. So ocean currents are linked to weather based on air masses. See how this works at the Smithsonian Weather Lab at this website.

Smithsonian Weather Lab 🔍

The military and the Weather Bureau pioneered the use of weather radar. In the late 1980s and 1990s, the U.S. government began using advanced ground-based Doppler weather radar systems. Initially, this was called NEXRAD, the abbreviation for Next-Generation Weather Radar. Today, it is called WSR-88D, for Weather Surveillance Radar 88 Doppler.

A variation is called dual-polarization radar, which uses both horizontal and vertical radio waves. Dual-polarization radar makes even more accurate predictions of precipitation and weather. Radar is useful in that it can make detections even when visibility is poor.

The weather satellite is another important tool that has been used in weather forecasting for more than 50 years. Satellites use remote sensing to scan the earth and the conditions in different areas.

The first meteorological satellite, called TIROS I, was launched into the atmosphere in 1960. TIROS I provided invaluable information and data. It also transmitted data faster than anything else had before it and with extreme accuracy.

The Doppler Effect

In 1842, an Austrian physicist proposed that there is a difference between the observed frequency of a wave and the emitted frequency of a wave when the observer is moving relative to the source of waves. The physicist was Christian Doppler (1803–1853). This observation was called the Doppler effect. Learn more about how Doppler radar works from the National Weather Service at this website.

NSSL's first research Doppler weather radar in 1973

photo credit: OAR/ERL/National Severe Storms Laboratory (NSSL)

NWS how radar works 🔍

But the satellites of today have little resemblance to those first satellites. Since the mid-1970s, NOAA and NASA have operated three Geostationary Operational Environmental Satellites (GOES). From approximately 22,307 miles above the equator, they gather information for more than half the earth.

The satellites take and transmit pictures of the earth every 15 minutes. They also measure the temperature of the clouds. Polar-orbiting satellites at about 500 to 600 miles above the poles also provide meteorological information.

In 2016, scientists introduced the latest generation of highly advanced geostationary weather satellites. The first of four GOES-R satellites was launched on November 26, 2016. These weather satellites will increase the accuracy and timeliness of forecasts with six new instruments.

After reaching its designated orbit two weeks after launch, the first satellite was named GOES-16. In addition to forecasting, GOES-16 will have search-and-rescue network capabilities.

More weather data comes from weather balloons. Twice a day, at locations around the world, weather balloons are launched into the atmosphere. Information also comes from surface weather stations and mobile stations on aircraft and ships.

Lots of data is fed into massive computer programs called numerical weather prediction models. The programs create computer analyses of global weather to pass on to national and regional weather centers.

METEOROLOGY CAREERS

Meteorologists use scientific principles to observe, explain, and forecast weather. Research meteorologists look at the relationship between the atmosphere, various environments, and life on Earth. They might concentrate on specific areas, such as severe storms or climate change. An operational forecaster uses research and data to make predictions about future weather.

Weather is everywhere, so meteorologists are, too! Meteorologists work at government agencies, weather stations, in broadcasting, and in many other industries.

- Military meteorologists make weather observations and forecasts for missions around the world.

- Aviation meteorologists help pilots and airports know what the weather will be like at take-off and along a flight path.

- Meteorologists work for city and county offices. They inform utility companies if severe weather could impact power needs and issue warnings if weather will impact public events.

Math and science are the most important subjects in meteorology. Computer programming and engineering are also useful. Meteorologists need at least a bachelor's degree in meteorology or another atmospheric science. Some meteorologists also have degrees in math, physics, and other physical sciences.

Many rewarding career opportunities are open to anyone who has knowledge and skills in meteorology and the atmospheric sciences.

Studying Hurricanes by Satellite

On December 15, 2016, NASA launched the first earth science small satellite constellation, the Cyclone Global Navigation Satellite System (CYGNSS). The CYGNSS mission will include eight small satellites that will show how and why winds in hurricanes and tropical cyclones intensify. CYGNSS will be able to see through the heavy rain of a hurricane to gather data about the storm's core.

Look at what young scientists at the University of Michigan are doing with the CYGNSS mission in this video.

CYGNSS students video

WOMEN IN METEOROLOGY

The number of women with STEM degrees and jobs has been steadily increasing since 2000. But many areas, such as meteorology, continue to show low numbers of women and minorities working in the field. According to the National Science Foundation, approximately 2,000 women, or 14 percent, are employed in the atmospheric sciences.

Why are the percentages so low?

The National Weather Service (NWS) is one of the largest employers of meteorologists. In 2014, the agency reported that 15 percent of its meteorologists were women. Female interns and forecasters numbered 22 percent each, but only 12 percent of lead forecasters were female.

Demonstrators get ready to launch weather balloons at a National Weather Center event

photo credit: Karen Bush Gibson

Mentoring

Many educators believe that the key to increasing diversity in STEM professions is through mentoring programs. Women and minorities in meteorology and other sciences can serve as role models for younger people. Seeing mentors succeed in their chosen fields helps girls and other underrepresented groups know that they can do it, too.

Yolanda Amadeo, the chief meteorologist for a Georgia television station, said that her mentors inspired her to be the best she could be. When she knew someone who had faced similar challenges to what she was facing, she believed she could overcome those challenges. Sharing experiences with a mentor made tough days a positive learning experience.

Now that she is established, Yolanda feels it's important to give back. She has mentored several aspiring meteorologists. Mentoring gives Yolanda a strong sense of satisfaction.

"I'm thrilled to share what I've learned from others and my own experience . . . . I'm always encouraging them not to sell themselves short and believe that they can be and do whatever their heart desires. It gives me so much joy to know that in some way what I said guided them and gave them the encouragement to pursue their dreams."

The National Science Foundation reports that 38.6 percent of undergraduate degrees in atmospheric sciences were earned by females in 2014. That number is actually down 3.6 percent from 10 years previously.

For both genders, 77.4 percent of undergraduate atmospheric science degrees are earned by white students. The leading organization for meteorologists, the American Meteorological Society, states that only 2 percent of its members are African American. However, the number of minority students is rising, particularly among Latino and Asian American students.

These numbers are expected to change as the career field continues to grow. Increasing numbers of employers are actively recruiting women and minorities for careers in meteorology. As more women enter the field of meteorology, more young girls will be able to find role models who look like them.

Let's meet three women working in meteorology today and hear their stories!

66 I feel like a kid in a candy store here in the National Weather Service. There is always an exciting science problem to solve and, as someone who has always loved weather, this is the place you want to be. 99

—Michelle Hawkins,
chief of the Severe, Fire, Public, and Winter Weather Services Branch at the National Weather Service

CHAPTER 2

Kelly Cass

What's your favorite type of weather? If your answer is snow, then you have a lot in common with Weather Channel meteorologist Kelly Cass. Growing up in upstate New York, she made lots of snow forts with her siblings. She still loves playing in the snow when skiing with her family. As a meteorologist, she's especially fascinated with something called lake-effect snow, which can result in large amounts of snowfall.

Lake-effect snow happens when cold air passes over the warmer waters of a lake. This can cause lake water to evaporate into the air, as though the air were a sponge picking up water. The now warmer air rises and then cools as it moves from the lake. If it's cold enough, the moisture in the air comes back down as snow. For Kelly, there's nothing more interesting!

CHILDHOOD DAYS

Kelly was born November 27, 1967, and grew up in the Hudson River Valley town of Poughkeepsie, New York. The Hudson River Valley includes towns and communities that sit along the Hudson River between the state capital in Albany and just north of New York City. Kelly's father worked for IBM and her mother stayed home to raise four children. Kelly was the oldest, with one brother and two sisters.

Science was always a part of Kelly's life. When she was in elementary school, she won first place in a science fair by demonstrating the effects of erosion on two patches of grass.

There are many questions about the natural world that Kelly suspected only science could answer. For example, Kelly often wondered why some winters have more snow than others. She thought a lot about this when she was a kid. She also wanted to know why summers brought thunderstorms.

As a young child, Kelly was scared of the sound of thunder. But once she learned that thunder was caused by the rapidly expanding air that surrounded lightning, she was no longer scared. Science helped her to overcome a fear, and Kelly's curiosity about the atmosphere grew.

Winter Storms

Winter storms present a special challenge for weather forecasters. Meteorologists must look at air temperature, lift, and moisture. Lift is the force that raises the moisture to form clouds. Warm air colliding with cold air can often result in lift. Temperatures in the clouds and near the ground make a big difference in what type of precipitation will fall. Knowledge of climate data, along with satellite and radar data, help meteorologists deliver accurate forecasts.

The main dangers from winter storms are traffic accidents on icy roads or exposure to the cold for an extended time. That's why it's so important for weather forecasters to get information about winter storms to the public.

Look at these NOAA examples of winter storms, the classic Nor'easter, and lake-effect snow.

NOAA winter forecasting 🔍

Cumulonimbus thunderstorm clouds forming in the background, with a smaller, low-level "scud" appearing in the foreground

photo credit: NOAA Photo Library, NOAA Central Library; OAR/ERL/National Severe Storms Laboratory (NSSL)

Kelly's mother helped her know that it was okay to be ambitious and to make mistakes along the way. Kelly said, "My mom would say, 'Nobody's perfect! Just keep learning and keep going!'"

In addition to her passion for science, Kelly also liked to play sports as a child, whether it was being part of a soccer team or playing whiffle ball with the neighborhood kids. Since the weather could affect those activities, Kelly made checking the weather forecast a regular thing.

COMMUNICATIONS AND METEOROLOGY

After high school, Kelly attended Dutchess Community College and received an associate's degree in communications. While at community college, she worked as an intern for an independent television station called WTZA.

Internships give students a chance to learn more about certain careers. College students often gain invaluable experience and knowledge as interns.

Cloud Challenge

How are you at naming clouds? Do you know the role clouds play in tropical storms? Try your hand at the Nova Labs Cloud Lab.

Cloud Lab PBS classify 🔍

For more about the role that clouds play in tropical storms, watch this Nova Labs video.

Nova Labs video 42 🔍

Armed with her associate's degree, Kelly went on to study abroad at Yonsei University in the South Korean capital city of Seoul. She earned a certificate in foreign studies through this program.

Established in 1885, Yonsei is the oldest university in South Korea. While there, Kelly learned about South Korean culture. She also studied tae kwon do and earned the advanced rank of red belt. Education in other countries offers a way to continue your studies while learning about other cultures. What do you think are some of the other benefits of going to school in a different country?

After spending a year in South Korea, Kelly returned to the United States and began work on her bachelor's degree in communications from Adelphi University. Adelphi is the oldest university on New York's Long Island. This was the next step on her path to discovering that her love of weather and her love of the media could blend to make a fulfilling career!

BROADCAST METEOROLOGY

When you think of a meteorologist, what comes to your mind? Many people think of someone who delivers weather forecasts for television or radio. Although meteorology includes many types of jobs, broadcast meteorologists are often the "face of meteorology." They serve a crucial function. They bring forecasts and warnings to the public and provide education about weather and climate.

The television station where Kelly first interned, WTZA, hired her as an associate producer after her graduation from Adelphi in 1990. Her duties included writing the weather report and designing weather maps. WTZA (now WRNN) served the middle Hudson River Valley and northern suburbs of New York City. Weather forecasts included the state capital of Albany and New York City.

> 66 My success in meteorology has been due to the encouragement from teachers and my parents, and the fact that I never felt it was abnormal for me, as a female, to pursue a career in science. I like to think that the outreach activities I participate in exposes youth and their parents to female scientists, such that their mental image of scientists includes women. 99
>
> **—Treena Jensen,**
> lead forecaster, Portland, Oregon, Weather Forecast Office

Kelly practiced delivering the weather so she'd be sure to get it right. One Memorial Day weekend, she got her first chance to be on camera. She reported on the weather and traffic along the New York State Thruway. She did such a good job that she was hired as a weekday weather anchor.

June Bacon-Bercey (1932–)

In the 1950s, only one African-American woman earned a degree in meteorology in the United States. Her name was June Bacon-Bercey. Born in Wichita, Kansas, on October 23, 1932, June was the only child born to an attorney and a music teacher. She liked to do what many girls like to do—bike riding, hiking, and being a Girl Scout.

June was interested in science as a kid, but attending the segregated schools of the time meant that she often wasn't encouraged and exposed to science. She would later say that growing up isolated helped her become more disciplined and a good student.

June worked as an engineer for the federal government. She held jobs with both the National Weather Service and the Atomic Energy Commission.

THE STORM OF THE CENTURY

After two years at WTZA, Kelly moved to WRGB-TV, the CBS affiliate station in Schenectady, New York. Her new job was the weekend weather anchor and reporter. She hadn't been there long when the Superstorm of 1993, also known as the "Storm of the Century," struck land.

She was approached about doing the weather on television, but she hesitated because of how female meteorologists were represented on television at the time. They were mostly shown as less smart and less capable than their male colleagues. However, she decided to give it a shot to show that women could be just as good at meteorology as men.

In 1970, June became a television meteorologist in Buffalo, New York. Two years later, she was the first woman and first African American to be awarded the American Meteorological Society's Seal of Approval for excellence in television weathercasting. She is a founding member of the American Meteorological Society Board on Women and Minorities. NASA also named June a Minority Pioneer for Achievement in Atmospheric Science. In 1979, she began working at NOAA as chief administrator of television activities.

This March blizzard produced record-breaking snow along the eastern United States from Maine to Alabama. There were even people in Florida who saw snow! The same storm produced thunderstorms and tornadoes in the South.

According to the National Weather Service, the 1993 superstorm dropped almost 13 cubic miles of snow on the United States. That's more than three times higher than North America's highest mountain, Mount Denali, which is 20,310 feet tall!

Airports and roads were closed because of blowing snow and little visibility. Schenectady was hit with 2 feet of snow, strong winds, and freezing temperatures. The road to Kelly's home was closed, so she spent a few nights at the TV station.

Kelly and the weather team provided around-the-clock coverage during the blizzard. The station earned an Associated Press award for outstanding newscast for their coverage of the 1993 blizzard. Kelly won the New York State Broadcasting Award for "Best Storm Coverage" and received her first television contract.

Kelly later earned a certificate in broadcast meteorology from Mississippi State University. Armed with an education in both communications and meteorology, Kelly was ready to share her love of meteorology with others.

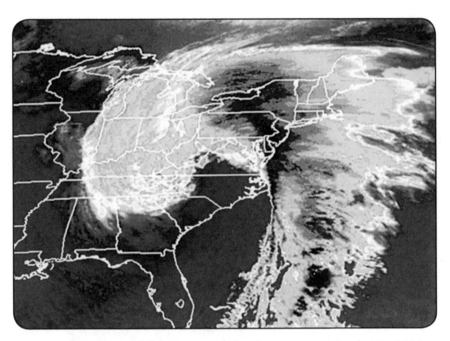

Satellite imagery of the "Storm of the Century" on March 13, 1993
photo credit: NOAA

ALL WEATHER ALL THE TIME

Where do you go most often for weather news in the United States? If you answered The Weather Channel, then you join approximately 158 million television and online viewers each month.

The Weather Channel started in 1982 as the first television station devoted to all weather all the time. Viewership often jumps 50 percent more when severe weather is in the forecast.

Hurricane Matthew

When Hurricane Matthew approached the East Coast during the first week of October in 2016, The Weather Channel provided 115 hours of live coverage during a period of five days. For two of those days, The Weather Channel was the top-watched cable network among viewers ages 25 to 54. It had a larger audience than CNN or Fox News.

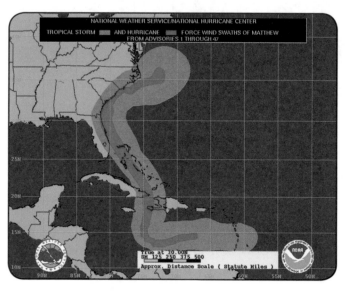

This graphic shows the scale of Hurricane Matthew in 2016

photo credit: NOAA

"I watched when The Weather Channel first launched back in the early '80s," says Kelly. "I was in middle school or high school at that time, and I remember watching Jeanetta Jones and being so impressed with her ability to talk about the weather in such a conversational way."

Kelly was offered a position at The Weather Channel in the late 1990s. It was a difficult decision for her to make, because The Weather Channel is based in Atlanta, Georgia.

If you've ever had to move to another state, you know how hard it is to leave family and friends. But Kelly knew that The Weather Channel was the best choice for her career as a broadcast meteorologist. She first appeared on-air at The Weather Channel in January 2000, and is now a popular member of the *AMHQ Weekend* show.

Ask & Answer

Television isn't the only way that people get their weather forecasts and news. What are some other ways of getting this information? Could there be a difference in the accuracy of different channels of information? How could you tell?

According to Kelly, the hardest part of her work day is when the alarm clock goes off at 2 a.m. But by the time she reaches work, she's ready to get started. At the studio, her day begins with getting her hair and make-up done around 3:30 a.m. Kelly uses her time in the make-up chair to get caught up on the latest news of the day.

She says, "I think that men in this business are given more of a pass when it comes to aging and appearance on air. Men can be balding, overweight, gray, etc. However, when a woman starts showing her age in wrinkles or gray hair, we typically get criticized, or worse, lose our jobs."

Kelly takes her duties as a broadcast meteorologist very seriously. Although Kelly makes it look effortless, she puts a lot of work into preparing for her time on the air. Television weather broadcasting often includes ad-libbing, or talking to viewers without a script. So Kelly must know what's going on in the world—in the weather and in the news. If she's doing any interviews, she also prepares interesting questions. Strong communication skills, both oral and written, are a must for broadcast meteorologists.

Kelly and the weather graphics producer go over the maps and animations that will be shown on-air. She also reviews the guide to the show, which is known as the news rundown. This tells Kelly what segments she's doing and where to be in the studio. The four-hour broadcast begins at 5 a.m.

Weather is always changing, so Kelly frequently checks the weather during the show. She knows people need to know not only about severe weather, but also how the weather might affect their daily plans. Occasionally, Kelly finds time to share her job through videos and pictures on her Facebook page.

Weather Graphics

One thing that has changed in approximately 75 years of television weather forecasting are the graphics. In the early days of weather broadcasts, weather forecasters pointed at maps. Then came the days of green screens and weather department-designed graphics, which were more interactive but still could be confusing for both viewers and broadcasters.

Weather graphics continue to evolve. Have you seen forecasters change the graphics by touching the screen in the same way you might manipulate your tablet or smartphone? The Weather Channel where Kelly works often uses interactive augmented reality to show the science of weather.

When you want to see satellite images, you don't have to wait for a newscast. You can see them any time at NOAA's Geostationary Satellite Server.

NOAA GOES 🔍

Flooding can be devastating, as shown in this photo
of flooding in Nashville, Tennessee, in 2010

Although she provides live forecasts for the weekend
show, severe weather sometimes demands more of her
time. When Texas experienced major flooding on
May 25 and 26, 2015, Kelly and fellow Weather
Channel meteorologist Mike Bettes broadcast for seven
hours!

Kelly enjoys opportunities that come her way as an
on-air weather personality. Sometimes, she's assigned
stories outside of live weather broadcasts.

These stories might relate to earth science in some
way, such as explaining flash flooding, the relationship
between climate change and health, or the science of
de-icing. One particularly fun assignment was getting
to fly in an F/A-18 jet with the U.S. Navy's Blue
Angels unit.

Kelly's academic background in communication serves her well as a broadcast meteorologist. She has a Seal of Approval from both the American Meteorological Society and the National Weather Association.

These Seals of Approval certify that Kelly has met the requirements and conditions to be recognized as a professional weather forecaster. They also require that she participate in continuing education opportunities.

Cool Careers:
Midnight Meteorologists

Weather is not a daytime or weekday event. Weather is constant, 24/7. Someone always needs to monitor the weather, so some meteorologists find themselves working the night shift. And we should be glad they do. In the Midwest, studies show that the strongest thunderstorms happen near midnight.

Most midnight meteorologists are compensated with somewhat higher pay, often called a shift differential. This is because working nights is not something many people want to do.

What about you? Do you think you would enjoy working a night shift? Can you see problems to this type of schedule? Are there any benefits?

Kelly is busy at home, too, with a husband, three children, and a shaggy sheepdog named Hobby. She's active in her community with her children's activities and community events.

Kelly and her family enjoy the outdoors, just as Kelly did when she was growing up. Sports such as soccer, softball, and tennis are popular in their house. So is outdoor recreation, including hiking and bike riding. Summers bring opportunities for boating and wakeboarding. But, of course, Kelly always checks the weather forecast first.

"Never stop being curious!" Kelly says. "That goes for all types of science, but especially meteorology. There is still so much to be learned and improved. I know we can do better with forecasting, and technology has allowed us to improve so much already."

Ask & Answer

Television broadcast meteorologists often become local celebrities. Why do you think this happens? What makes viewers feel connected to their meteorologists?

CHAPTER 3

Bianca Hernandez

While Bianca Hernandez doesn't remember it, her first experiences of the world happened while her town was recovering from the onslaught of Hurricane Andrew, a category 5 hurricane. Hurricane Andrew caused severe damage in several states, including Florida, where Bianca was born on September 24, 1992, just about a month after Hurricane Andrew hit. The Hernandez family was living in a mobile home in Miami that Hurricane Andrew damaged.

Bianca grew up hearing stories and watching home videos of this significant storm. "My mom has always told me that by the time I was four, I was already in love with the weather and intrigued by it, and I just knew. It's weird, because as I grew older, that never changed," says Bianca.

Summer afternoons in Florida often bring rain. Tropical systems made Bianca want to be outside so that she could watch the storms. "Whenever we had any tropical system, I wanted to be outside watching and listening to the storms. The last thing I wanted to do was observe from the inside."

During hurricane season, from June to November, the family had to use hurricane shutters on the windows. These keep the glass from breaking during high winds. All year round, the weather was something to think about and prepare for.

> 66 I grew up on a five-generation farm in Missouri, so I understood the importance of accurate weather information very early. Weather impacts everyone and everything. There is no other field that has such a broad and diverse mission. 99
>
> **—Laura Furgione,**
> deputy assistant administrator for weather services and the deputy director of the National Weather Service

Andrew Strikes

A tropical storm named Andrew developed from a tropical wave off the African coast. By the time Tropical Storm Andrew reached the Bahamas, it had been upgraded to a hurricane because its wind speeds exceeded 74 miles per hour.

Hurricane Andrew was intense when it made landfall at Homestead on the southeastern tip of Florida. It crossed the state just south of Miami to reach the Gulf of Mexico. Wind speeds had decreased by the time it made a second landfall in southeastern Louisiana, before dissipating.

The worst damage from Hurricane Andrew was in South Florida. Storm surges reached up to 16.9 feet. Homes, businesses, crops, coastal reefs, and the Everglades were all damaged. Hurricane Andrew was one of the top five costliest hurricanes in U.S. history.

Dadeland Mobile Home Park after Hurricane Andrew

Bianca's mother, Francie Pages, taught Bianca how to count the seconds between the flash of lightning and the clap of thunder to find out how far away the lightning originated. Light travels almost instantaneously, but sound takes about one second to travel 1,000 feet. Since a mile is 5,280 feet, it takes thunder about five seconds to travel a mile.

If you count to less than five seconds between the thunder and lightning, the storm is closer than a mile. More than five seconds, and it's farther than a mile.

Hurricanes and tropical storms were part of Bianca's childhood. While many young children watched cartoons, Bianca watched The Weather Channel. It was often the first thing she watched in the morning and the last thing she watched at night.

More About Hurricanes

Take a virtual tour of the National Hurricane Center here.
national hurricane
John Ferrante 🔎

You can also see the paths that hurricanes through history have taken in this link to Historical Hurricane Tracks from the NOAA Coastal Services Center.
NOAA historical tracks 🔎

Cloud-to-ground and cloud-to-cloud lightning strikes during a night-time thunderstorm

photo credit: NOAA Photo Library, NOAA Central Library; OAR/ERL/NSSL

Bianca wondered what it would be like to work for the National Hurricane Center (NHC) or the National Weather Service. Established in 1965, the NHC shares space and resources with the National Weather Service Forecast Office for Miami-South Florida. The NHC delivers forecasts about threatening tropical weather. It also analyzes storms to learn more about hurricanes in order to save lives.

Soon after she turned eight years old, Bianca and her family moved to Raleigh, North Carolina, where her stepfather worked as a psychiatrist. Her mother was a stay-at-home mom. Bianca has two step-brothers, a half-sister, and a half-brother.

North Carolina is no stranger to hurricanes or tropical storms. Their National Hockey League team is even called the Carolina Hurricanes.

OFF TO SCHOOL

No one was surprised when Bianca went to Florida State University to study meteorology. She also decided to minor in mathematics. Meteorology isn't just about the science of the atmosphere—it's also about taking measurements and looking for patterns.

Math is very useful for meteorologists. According to the American Meteorological Society, mathematics is a language that can describe things that happen in the world. No matter what country you're from and what language you know how to speak, through math, you can communicate with people all around the world.

Ask & Answer

Have you ever thought of math as a language? How do meteorologists use mathematics as a language to describe things that happen in the atmosphere?

When she was a college sophomore, Bianca applied to be a student volunteer at the Tallahassee Weather Forecast Office. She was very disappointed when she didn't get chosen. "After, I went to the office and asked them what I had to do in order to be eligible and, from that point on, it was history!"

Bianca did become a volunteer in the Tampa National Weather Service office. She was there when Tropical Storm Andrea hit Florida's west coast in June 2013. Her experiences during Tropical Storm Andrea taught her a lot about tropical storms.

A tropical storm is the category of storm between a tropical depression and a hurricane. A tropical depression is a storm just forming, with wind speeds up to 38 miles per hour. A hurricane has winds stronger than 74 miles per hour. When a storm is upgraded to a tropical storm, when it has winds above 38 miles per hour, that's when it's named.

"Tropical Storm Andrea hit the west coast of Florida," she says. "That night was so exciting, I didn't want to leave! I even asked if I could stay longer! This was the event that made me certain that I wanted a career with the National Weather Service."

Ask & Answer

Have you ever been disappointed when you weren't chosen for something you really wanted to do? How did you handle it?

Bianca shared important information about the impacts of Tropical Storm Andrea in an interview with the Spanish language network, Univision. Being able to learn about a storm and communicate what she learned to a wider audience made her feel useful. It was something she knew she wanted to do more of.

While at college, Bianca's volunteer work with the National Weather Service forecast offices often meant delivering weather information through social media and radio stations. She even did live briefings for amateur radio operators, or ham operators. As a student meteorologist, she informed the public about weather watches and warnings on the local Tallahassee television network, 4FSU.

For Bianca, volunteer work was a crucial part of becoming a meteorologist. She can't say enough good things about it! She suggests that if you are interested in meteorology, you should definitely volunteer with local emergency managers or a weather forecast office.

What's in a Name?

Andrew, Katrina, Sandy—have you heard these names in reference to something other than people? These are all names of Atlantic hurricanes! Names are easier to remember than longitude and latitude readings. In 1953, the United States began naming hurricanes using women's names. This lasted until 1979, when both male and female names began to be used.

Today, the National Hurricane Center maintains a list of names for tropical storms and hurricanes in the Atlantic Ocean and Gulf of Mexico. The list follows a procedure set up by the World Meteorological Organization. The first storm of the season always starts with an A, the second with a B, and so on. The first storm of 2018 will be named Alberto, and the name Andrea will introduce the 2019 tropical storm season. The only letters that are not used are Q, U, X, Y, and Z. If there are more than 21 storms in a season, then names will start with letters from the Greek alphabet.

When a storm has been particularly deadly and costly, the name of that storm is retired from the list. By early 2016, 80 names, including Andrew, had been retired and replaced with new names by the World Meteorological Organization.

In addition to volunteering during college, Bianca had an internship with the NOAA Aircraft Operations Center. She led weather briefings with Aircraft Operations employees so they knew how the weather might impact them. She also had the opportunity to work on different scientific projects, such as testing what happens to dropwindsondes in extreme winds.

A dropwindsonde, also called a dropsonde, is a cylinder-shaped instrument that sends information about its surroundings, including temperature, pressure, winds, and humidity. Dropwindsondes are released from aircraft above a storm. A parachute keeps it from falling too quickly.

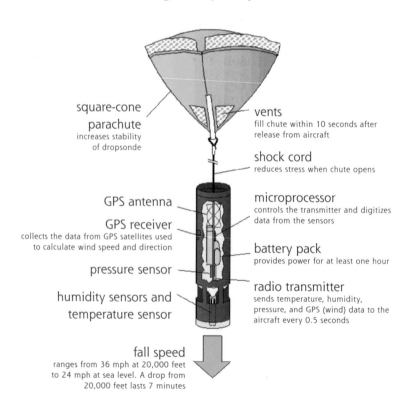

square-cone parachute
increases stability of dropsonde

vents
fill chute within 10 seconds after release from aircraft

shock cord
reduces stress when chute opens

GPS antenna

GPS receiver
collects the data from GPS satellites used to calculate wind speed and direction

microprocessor
controls the transmitter and digitizes data from the sensors

pressure sensor

battery pack
provides power for at least one hour

humidity sensors and temperature sensor

radio transmitter
sends temperature, humidity, pressure, and GPS (wind) data to the aircraft every 0.5 seconds

fall speed
ranges from 36 mph at 20,000 feet to 24 mph at sea level. A drop from 20,000 feet lasts 7 minutes

Bianca standing outside a P3 after storm chasing
photo provided by Bianca Hernandez

Bianca was the lead author of a research project on dropwindsondes in extreme wind environments. She presented the research at the 94th American Meteorological Society meeting in 2014.

Although presenting to weather professionals might be intimidating to a college student, Bianca's experience in presenting briefings to NOAA employees and her volunteer work with weather forecast offices helped. "Due to being female and my looks, people always just thought of me as another 'TV weather girl.' So I had to work hard to prove to my classmates and professors that I had what it took to be a scientist."

EMERGENCY SERVICES

After graduating with a bachelor of science in meteorology in 2014, Bianca began working as an assistant state meteorologist for the Florida Division of Emergency Management. Meteorology isn't just about studying and observing severe weather. It's also about obtaining and interpreting information for other people.

Susan Solomon

When Susan Solomon (1956–) was 10 years old, she saw a television show called *The Undersea World of Jacques Cousteau*. The show, with its focus on ocean life, fascinated her. But when Susan took a high school biology class, she realized that she didn't enjoy the subject as much as she'd expected. She switched her focus to chemistry and found herself excited about the data—she was especially interested in the atmosphere.

After earning her doctorate at the University of California at Berkeley, she began working at NOAA's Aeronomy Laboratory in Boulder, Colorado. A pioneer in the study of atmospheric ozone in the Antarctic, she played a key role in the 1989 global ban on chemicals that were destroying atmospheric ozone and creating human health problems.

It means designing emergency procedures to have in place and helping people access emergency services. Have you heard of the Federal Emergency Management Agency (FEMA)? FEMA is a federal agency that provides assistance in the case of disaster. Every state also has an emergency management agency.

As a senior scientist with NOAA, Susan's work includes increasing our knowledge of the stratosphere. She also works as a professor at the Massachusetts Institute of Technology, where she is able to impart her own knowledge and excitement about science to future meteorologists and climate scientists. She says, "I find it wonderful to be able to talk about those results with ordinary people of all kinds, with children. . . . The natural curiosity of people is where I think we can start a good conversation."

States have disaster plans in place that dictate how the population should respond to likely emergencies. In Florida, weather is a huge part of planning for potential disasters.

Bianca monitored and interpreted weather events to help Florida's agencies be better prepared to respond to and recover from significant weather, such as tropical storms and hurricanes. In addition to working with Florida forecast offices and the State Emergency Operations Center, she coordinated efforts with FEMA and the governor's office.

Bianca also participated in outreach activities so people could become more weather-ready and knowledgeable. Bianca explains the 30-30 rule for lightning strikes: "If the seconds between seeing lightning and hearing lightning are fewer than 30 seconds, people should seek shelter immediately. Then, remain in shelter for 30 minutes after the last sound of thunder." When people know what to do during an emergency weather event, there are far fewer injuries.

Ask & Answer

Do you have a home or school emergency plan in case of a natural disaster? What are the main points of the plan? What is a good way to come up with a plan or improve the plan you have?

A monsoon storm in southern Arizona

photo credit: NOAA Weather in Focus Photo Contest 2015

REALIZING A CHILDHOOD DREAM

In June 2015, Bianca began working for the National Weather Service at the Phoenix, Arizona, weather forecast office. The Phoenix office is one of 122 NWS forecast offices. Its forecast area is south-central and southwest Arizona, as well as southeast California.

By moving from Florida to Arizona, Bianca moved from hurricanes to monsoons! She exchanged climates, too. She went from a wet, humid environment to Arizona's dry climate.

Bianca Hernandez 65

The National Weather Service

The NWS was established as the Weather Bureau in 1870. In 1970, several earth science agencies combined under the National Oceanic and Atmospheric Administration (NOAA). The Weather Bureau became the National Weather Service and part of NOAA. Today, the NWS is based in Silver Spring, Maryland. It has six regional headquarters, nine national centers, 13 river forecast offices, and 122 weather forecast offices. With approximately 5,000 employees, the NWS collects about 76 billion observations each year. It issues approximately 50,000 warnings and 1.5 million forecasts.

Woman with the Weather Bureau tracking radiosonde balloons, probably around WWII

photo credit: NOAA Photo Library

66 The rate at which technology is changing is as extreme as our climate. No matter what you do, you need STEM. As society continues to transform, so will science. 99

—Eleanor Bell,
principal meteorologist at The Weather Company

A monsoon is a seasonal shift in the wind that can bring wet or dry storms. In North America, monsoons arrive in the summer. Winds shift from west or northwest to southwest. This brings moisture from the Pacific. Mexico is usually the hardest hit, but U.S. states such as New Mexico and Arizona can be affected as well.

Monsoon season officially begins when the dew point averages at least 55 degrees for three days in a row. As the day heats up, warm air and humidity rise. When the air condenses, violent thunderstorms and flooding can occur. The trick is knowing what areas will be affected. One area can flood while another remains completely dry.

Bianca can figure out the probable flood areas in her forecast area by analyzing 291 flood points. To do this, she uses a geospatial mapping program called ArcMap. The average output from monsoon season in Phoenix is 2 to 3 inches of rain a year. This might not sound like much, but flooding is likely anytime the rainfall produces more water than the ground can soak up.

A forecast office has several teams of NWS meteorologists. The Phoenix office has a public forecast team that's responsible for the weather forecast for up to seven days. Members focus on temperatures, precipitation chances, and sky cover.

Bianca works with the decision support services (DSS) team, which coordinates information with other agencies and partners. She starts most of her work days by analyzing current weather and model data to see what conditions may affect the forecast area. During monsoon season, the NWS forecast office adds a radar and assistant radar/weather coordinator position. The duties of this job include tracking and timing monsoons, a task Bianca enjoys.

As a member of the DSS team, Bianca has built relationships with many different groups, including area emergency managers and state government agencies. Together, the different agencies can work to predict hazardous weather and keep the population safe.

66 Any comparison between the way it was when I started and the way it is now is like comparing the covered wagon with a jet plane. 99

—Joanne Simpson,
meteorologist, speaking about changes in
meteorology for women

Cool Careers:
Incident Meteorologist

Every year, wildfires burn an average of 7 million acres of land in the United States. Hardest hit is the western United States. Thousands of homes and businesses are destroyed, with annual costs up to $2 billion. People can die in the wildfires or suffer health problems from the smoke.

Incident meteorologists (IMETs) often work for the NWS. These specialists on weather and wildfires work with fire control agencies, the Forest Service, and anyone affected by wildfires. In cases of major wildfires, IMETs travel to the site to interpret the weather and evaluate its affect on the wildfire. For example, thunderstorms often release more lightning than rain, and lightning is a major contributor to wildfires.

IMETs also need to be aware of terrain changes and how that can affect the wildfire. Remote automated weather stations are placed around the fire to provide ground observations to the IMET. Fire crews are given regular briefings so that they know what to expect. An IMET at a wildfire sets up at the command center and usually remains for a two-week shift or until the fire is contained, whichever happens first.

Unlike many older female professionals, Bianca hasn't experienced challenges due to her gender in her career. She finds that role models and mentors are chosen based on their meteorology expertise, not gender. Perhaps, future meteorologists will have the same experiences as Bianca.

REACHING OUT

"Working for the National Weather Service as a meteorologist means your schedule is very far from what society takes as 'normal.' My days and weeks are never the same!" Bianca says. "Our office is open 24/7, 365 days a year, which means I work days, nights, overnights, weekends, and holidays."

In addition to accomplishing her routine duties, Bianca also serves as a team leader for the diversity and social media teams in her office.

It's not enough to communicate warnings to just emergency and government partners. Everyone needs to receive weather information in a timely manner. About 30 percent of the residents in the Phoenix forecast area speak Spanish as their first language. Bianca provides information to the Spanish language network, Telemundo, and for the deaf and hard-of-hearing community.

Bianca knows how crucial it is to reach the maximum number of people with weather information. Bianca's second language is Spanish. She's passionate about her Cuban heritage.

As part of the NWS Spanish outreach team, Bianca and about nine others working at NWS offices across the country translate brochures and materials for Spanish-speaking audiences. The team also records informational videos.

Spanish and English

If you live in an area where only one language is usually spoken, it can be easy to forget that not everyone understands that language. Why is it important to make information available in different languages?

You can watch Bianca explain the impact of a weather phenomenon called El Niño to the Spanish-speaking community in this FEMA YouTube video. Can you understand any of the words?

Bianca Hernandez El Niño video

When she's not analyzing and reporting the weather, Bianca likes to go hiking. Arizona boasts a number of trails, and Bianca is always searching for a new trail to try. She also likes to travel. Her goal is to visit two new cities every year.

In the future, Bianca would like to become a warning coordination meteorologist (WCM), the face of decision support services. Since she loves communicating about the weather and its hazards to others, Bianca thinks this would be a good fit for her. She says, "A WCM is pretty much the expert when it comes to decision support services. You have a lot of knowledge about all of our partners and all of our partners' needs."

Bianca is happy to be a part of the meteorological profession, and feels her career has been a natural progression from her early beginnings in a hurricane.

CHAPTER 4

Pamela Heinselman

What if you could tell when and where severe weather was going to strike? Would increased warning times help people get to safety before disastrous weather struck? Dr. Pamela Heinselman, a research meteorologist with the NOAA National Severe Storms Laboratory, has spent her adult life working on those two questions. Whether she's hiking in the woods or discovering better ways of forecasting weather, Pam funnels her fascination with the natural world into improving the relationship between humans and nature.

Pam was born January 31, 1970, in Kansas City, Missouri. Before she reached one year old, her family moved to Maryland. Pam calls the northern Maryland town of Westminster her childhood home. She was the middle child of three and the only girl born to Don and Dianne Heinselman. Pam's father worked for the Social Security Administration, while her mother stayed home to care for the children when they were young.

Pam's parents stressed the importance of being well-rounded in education and extracurricular activities. In addition to exploring the woods behind her house, Pam enjoyed playing sports, such as softball. She also spent time learning and practicing the piano.

Pam's mother tells a story of a young Pam walking home from the bus stop and being annoyed with the raindrops that kept clinging to her coat. Annoyance turned to fascination when Pam took her first earth science course in eighth grade. It was the first science class that really excited her. Meteorology was only a small part of the curriculum, but it was enough for Pam. She looked at the skies with new interest and appreciation.

Do you ever look at the sky and try to name a cloud? When a storm is moving in, are you fascinated by the changing sky? As a girl, Pam really enjoyed observing cloud formations and the changing weather. She would make predictions based on her observations—different types of clouds indicate different types of weather.

Have you ever done science projects? When Pam was young, she made her own barometer, an instrument that tracks air pressure over time. A barometer showing rising air pressure means the weather will be sunny and dry. Falling air pressure means wet weather is on its way. Pam says, "Anything hands-on that relates to the world is a great way to learn more about science!"

Pam's parents always encouraged her interests. They, along with her teachers, supported her decision to be a meteorologist. Pam was lucky to have the support she needed to go far in her field.

A METEOROLOGY EDUCATION

After graduating from high school, Pam moved to Missouri to attend St. Louis University. This is a top U.S. research university with a small meteorology program.

Ask & Answer

Have you ever entered a science fair? Science fairs are events where students gather to present the experiments they conducted. Sometimes, local scientists judge science fairs, so it's also a way to meet actual scientists!

During Pam's time there, the program reached a milestone. Equal numbers of male and female students were enrolled in the atmospheric sciences program. Historically, women have been in the minority in college science programs. Knowing that there was a large number of female students working in the same field as her created a sense of community for Pam.

In 1992, Pam graduated with honors and a bachelor of science in earth and atmospheric sciences. Two years later, she earned a master of science in earth and atmospheric sciences, also from St. Louis University.

Pam's focus in graduate school was on climate-scale phenomena, such as El Niño. She started a PhD program in climate dynamics, but after a semester, realized it wasn't for her. Pam decided to join the workforce, which took her to one of the top locations in the country for severe weather research and technology—Norman, Oklahoma.

Ask & Answer

Pam felt a sense of community with the large group of females in her college meteorology program. How does this feeling of belonging to a group help when you're in school? Why is it helpful to know other female students studying the same subject as you?

The National Severe Storm Laboratory's first Doppler weather radar was located in Norman, Oklahoma, in the 1970s

photo credit: NOAA Photo Library, NOAA Central Library; OAR/ERL/NSSL

RESEARCH SCIENCE

A small city in central Oklahoma, Norman is home to the University of Oklahoma (OU). In the 1970s, the university partnered with NOAA and other weather-focused institutions, including the National Weather Center and the National Severe Storms Laboratory, for meteorological research.

When Pam first arrived in Norman at the beginning of 1995, she worked as a research associate with the Cooperative Institute for Mesoscale Meteorological Studies (CIMMS). This joint NOAA/OU research organization was created in 1978 to improve understanding of mesoscale meteorological phenomena, weather radar, and regional climate.

Her job was to help develop and test severe storm-tracking algorithms. "During the next three years, I found myself more interested in the severe storms research being done by PhD scientists at the NOAA National Severe Storms Laboratory [NSSL] and exploring ways to get involved," Pam says.

Pam became part of the severe weather warning and technology transfer team. Her work focused on storm cells, especially their characteristics and the role they play in storm forecasts. A storm cell is a mass of air that contains currents that move up and down. This is the smallest storm-producing system.

Pam's group worked to improve the performance of the WSR-88D Storm Cell Identification and Tracking Algorithm. You might have heard of WSR-88D by a different name—Doppler.

Doppler radar uses shorts bursts of radio waves that bounce off water particles in the atmosphere. The change in frequency of the returned signal shows the velocity of these particles relative to the radar location. Information from Doppler radar is used to determine the direction and speed of a storm.

> 66 Meteorology is a rare profession—romantic and independent of political influence—which allows consistent and interesting work. 99
>
> **—Vida Auguliene,**
> director of the Lithuanian Hydrometeorological Service,
> vice president of the World Meteorological Organization

Twister!

During the early 1980s, NSSL/OU researchers placed TOTO (TOtable Tornado Observatory)

in the path of an oncoming tornado to measure temperature, pressure, and relative humidity. The movie *Twister*, starring Helen Hunt and Bill Paxton, was a fictionalized account of this. You can watch the preview here.

TOTO

photo credit: NOAA Photo Library, NOAA Central Library; OAR/ERL/NSSL

Twister movie preview 🔍

Pam didn't have any female role models, but three male scientists encouraged her to return to school to earn a PhD in meteorology. A PhD is the highest academic degree you can achieve. Her research and dissertation topic was on the variability of summer storm development over central Arizona. Forecasting weather is always challenging, but the mountains and deserts of central Arizona make it even harder.

Upon receiving her degree in 2004, Pam again began considering where she wanted to go with her career. "At this point, I was the only female scientist in the radar division I worked in. I was one of the few meteorologists working among electrical engineers and software developers. At that time, I felt like a duck out of water and wasn't sure whether I wanted to stay or find a job elsewhere. My feeling of not fitting in was driven mostly by the realization that I prefer working with people and doing big-picture thinking more than working alone and performing detailed analyses."

PHASED-ARRAY RADAR

Weather forecasts come from a variety of sources, including observation, satellite images, and computerized weather models. Radar is another important source of meteorological information. Radar data is helpful in understanding severe storms, such as tornadoes, hail, and high-wind events. Using radar to improve forecast models can make a big difference in forecasts.

At the time Pam was considering her career direction, a phased array radar once used by the U.S. Navy was being installed at NSSL. A meteorologist was needed to explore its severe-weather capabilities.

Pam says, "I stepped up to the plate and shared my interest with my boss. He gave me the green light and asked me to go forth and 'do great things.'"

Supercell thunderstorms over the Plains produce many tornadoes
photo credit: Sean Waugh NOAA/NSSL

Pam began using the NOAA Hazardous Weather Testbed to experiment with phased-array radar. The Hazardous Weather Testbed, located in the National Weather Center, provides a way for scientists to test and evaluate new models and technologies.

Traditional weather radar, such as Doppler radar, is steered mechanically and collects data every five minutes. Phased-array radar speedily scans the atmosphere with electronically steered beams. It allows users to quickly find rapidly evolving severe weather.

With four radar antennas, phased-array radar can sample an area in less than a minute. This is five to six times faster than the current radar generally being used.

Weather Radar

People are constantly trying to invent new technology to improve human life. Phased-array radar is simply one more example of human innovation! You can watch Pam explain phased-array radar in this National Severe Storms Laboratory video.

nssl bite-sized hands-on 🔎

By saving that time, forecasters can warn people of impending bad weather sooner. The installation of a phased-array radar on loan from the U.S. Navy allowed Pam and other researchers to develop and explore its uses for severe weather. Information gleaned from this new radar about pre-storm events suggested it could be helpful for forecasting.

In 2010, Phased-Array Radar Innovative Sensing Experiment (PARISE) was born. PARISE allows NWS forecasters to interact with rapid-scan radar data to discover the effects on lead time and the accuracy of forecasts. PARISE results were significant.

In 2012, using phased-array radar data, forecasters provided an average tornado forecast lead-time of 20 minutes, which was more than twice the amount of advance notice from traditional data. In addition, false alarms dropped with the use of phased-array data.

In 2013, researchers looked at differences in 1-minute and 5-minute phased-array radar updates. The 1-minute update experimental group had a mean lead-time of 21.5 minutes, while the 5-minute update control group had a 17.3 mean lead-time.

Another PARISE experiment launched in 2015 helped create timelines of the decision-making process in issuing weather warnings. The timelines were analyzed to determine how forecasters use phased-array radar data.

Based on her research, Pam believes that phased-array radar will improve the lead times of weather warnings. It will also decrease false alarms and improve forecasters' performances.

PRESIDENTIAL RECOGNITION

In 2009, Pam received some very exciting news. She had won a Presidential Early Career Award for Scientists and Engineers (PECASE), one of the most prestigious awards for scientists.

Established by President Bill Clinton in 1996, the U.S. government recognizes and honors scientists early in their career with this award. Pam was honored for her work in improving forecasting through new radar systems. PECASE confirmed to Pam that she was on the right career path and it boosted her confidence. The award opened doors to other opportunities, particularly in leadership.

Phased-array radar such as at this Air Force base has long been used by the military. Now, Pam and the NSSL researchers have found applications for weather forecasting.

photo credit: U.S. Air Force

The award also included financial compensation, which Pam used to help a graduate student she was advising. The student was Pam's first female graduate student. Higher education is very expensive, and Pam's financial award made it possible for the student to earn her master of science in meteorology.

PECASE is a significant award, but it's not the only one Pam has received. Early in her career, she received a Bronze Medal from CIMMS and a Silver Medal from the U.S. Department of Commerce for improvements to Next Generation Radar (NEXRAD) severe-weather-detection algorithms and system.

An important part of being a scientist affiliated with a university is the publication of research. Pam has been published dozens of times and has been recognized twice by NOAA for outstanding scientific papers.

In 2010, Pam won the Professor Dr. Vilho Väisälä Award from the World Meteorological Organization. Vilho Väisälä (1889–1969) was a noted twentieth-century meteorologist and physicist from Finland. The award is given for outstanding research papers on instruments and observation methods.

PARISE-EyeT

Time is important when you are forecasting severe weather. The capabilities of phased-array radar are exciting, but that's a lot of data in front of a human. What do forecasters look at? What do they not see? Katie Bowden, a PhD student working with Pam, researched eye-tracking during the 2015 PARISE experiments. Eye-tracking research is used in medical and air traffic professions to understand how people take in information. Evaluating how forecasters track and use data can help improve forecast techniques. It might also lead to more user-friendly tools. You can learn more about this eye-tracking research in weather in this video.

Katie Bowden eye tracking video 🔍

WARN-ON-FORECAST

After 10 years of leading the phased-array research program, Pam decided to move from radar research to the forecast research development division in late 2016. She became the acting program manager for a new program called Warn-On-Forecast.

Joanne Simpson

Joanne Simpson (1923–2010) grew up in Boston, Massachusetts, near the ocean. Joanne enjoyed sailing a single-sail catboat off nearby Cape Cod. She often watched the clouds while sailing. But it wasn't until she entered the University of Chicago during World War II that she became excited about science and took her first course in meteorology. She loved the class so much that she went on to get a master's degree in the field, and began to work toward her PhD. However, her faculty advisor discouraged her because no women had ever completed a PhD in meteorology before. Joanne ignored him, and found someone willing to be her PhD advisor. Her work took place before the time of weather satellites. Joanne drew detailed maps of cloud formations to show the role of tropical clouds in global atmospheric circulation. Until then, it was believed that clouds were a result, not a cause, of weather.

The goal of Warn-On-Forecast is to increase lead times for severe weather warnings. Pam's new position places her in a leadership role to focus on the big picture. "I really enjoy working with people and bringing expertise to the weather service that can help save lives and help people protect themselves and their property."

Joanne became the first woman to earn a PhD in meteorology. Because of her gender, she had trouble finding a job. Eventually, she was able to find work as a professor, and later began working for the Weather Bureau, which would eventually become part of NOAA. She led the Experimental Meteorology Laboratory and was awarded the Department of Commerce Gold Medal in 1972. In 2002, Joanne Simpson became the first woman awarded the International Meteorological Organization Prize.

Ask & Answer

Have you ever taken on a leadership role, perhaps with a class project? What qualities do you think make a good leader?

Currently, NWS issues warnings by looking at the conditions in the environment—temperature, humidity, and air pressure. Meteorologists look at what's going on within a storm system. There are precursors, such as storm height and intensity, that helps forecasters look forward in time to what the storm is going to do during the next half hour.

When certain precursors are present, NWS will issue a warning. This is called Warn-On-Detection. Pam and her team expect phased-array research will help with the development of a high-resolution model to forecast even earlier, up to an hour ahead of time, without waiting for those precursors.

66 I've wanted to be a meteorologist since age 4. My passion has never wavered and was only confirmed when a tornado struck without warning in Huntsville, Alabama, on November 15, 1989. I wanted to . . . help prevent something like that from happening again. 99

—Krissy Hurley,
warning coordination meteorologist

Forecasting Models

No one can predict the future with absolute certainty. That goes for the weather, too! Weather is predicted through observation, trends, and statistics. Sometimes predictions are right, sometimes they're wrong. Meteorologists seek to improve the accuracy of forecasts with computerized weather models that take in various data, particularly mathematical data that looks at relationships between variables. Many computer models engage in a simulation, a "what if" scenario. Using an algorithm, the computer model provides a likely forecast.

Warn-On-Forecast will be the latest and most accurate forecasting model available. Learn more in this National Severe Storms Laboratory video.

nssl video bite-sized forecast 🔍

While everyone benefits from earlier forecasts, it becomes even more of an issue for large public groups. What if a tornado is on a path toward a hospital? The hospital needs time to move patients to safety. What if a storm is threatening a national or college-level football game with up to 100,000 people attending? A longer lead time helps bring people to safety. Warn-On-Forecast will protect more people and property from severe weather than ever before.

When not working, Pam likes being physically active, whether it's walking her dog or taking exercise classes. Pam always enjoys dancing. One of her favorite things to do is ballroom dancing with her husband.

GUIDING AND MENTORING

Pam added adjunct assistant professor at OU's School Meteorology to her list of jobs in 2008. Teaching and guiding younger people interested in meteorology is a natural fit for her.

Currently, she advises graduate students on their academic path, including helping them choose courses and research projects. She has also mentored undergraduate students on summer research projects.

Pam knows the importance of education and is an educator in many other ways, too. She educates the public about weather radar at National Weather Center events. She also provides job shadowing experiences for emerging female scientists.

Ask & Answer

Why is it important for women to be encouraged to go into STEM fields such as meteorology, fields that historically women have not been a large part of?

Cool Careers: Meteorological Technology Developer

Forecasting, broadcasting, and research meteorologists use specialized instruments and technology to do their jobs. Who's creating that technology? Meteorological technology developers can be meteorologists, engineers, or computer programmers. What unites them is the goal of inventing new technology to improve the science of meteorology.

Instrumentation technology involves the development and manufacturing of complex instruments, as well as ongoing technology support and maintenance. Many companies specialize in the design and building of atmospheric instrumentation, which may be simple or extremely complex. Users are home owners, universities, and weather agencies. What's the next technology in meteorology?

Pam is grateful to the scientists who encouraged her to earn a PhD in meteorology. When she found herself the only female in her division and one of the few meteorologists working among electrical engineers and software developers, she recalls feeling like a duck out of water. But the support she received helped her find her place in meteorology. She believes all women should receive that same support.

Science involves more than working in a lab. It can also mean working with people, both peers and the public. Pam often travels to collaborate with other meteorologists and to speak at conferences. She is in high demand at conferences that encourage young women in STEM careers.

One of the messages Pam wants girls interested in science to know is the importance of being authentic and true to yourself. Look for opportunities to engage with scientists. Many are happy to answer questions or give tours. Weather centers and forecast offices often give tours too. It's never too early to learn about science. "It is a journey filled with unexpected twists and turns that led to where I am and what I am doing today."

66 Today, three of my female mentees are enrolled in a PhD meteorology program, one of them about to complete her degree . . . . For me, this clearly shows the importance of supporting women's interest in science, and identifying female scientist role models, as you can't be what you can't see. 99

—Nelsie Ramos,
meteorologist with NOAA National Hurricane Center
Tropical Analysis and Forecast Branch

300 BCE

- Chinese astronomers create a calendar dividing the year into 24 festivals, each focusing on a different type of weather.

340 BCE

- Aristotle writes *Meteorologica* about his theories on weather.

1464

- Nicholas Cusa invents the first known weather instrument, the hygrometer, which measured humidity.

1648

- Blaise Pascal demonstrates that atmospheric pressure decreases with increasing altitude.

1686

- Edmond Halley publishes the first comprehensive map of trade winds.

1802

- Luke Howard first classifies clouds by type.

1845

- The telegraph is invented.

1849

- The Smithsonian Institution supplies weather instruments to telegraph companies.

1860s

- Weather-observing stations appear after the invention of the telegraph, which makes it easier and faster to share information.

1870

- The Weather Bureau is established when Congress directs military stations to take meteorological observations.

1890

- The weather service is transferred to a civilian government agency under the Department of Agriculture. It is named the U.S. Weather Bureau.

1892

- The widespread use of weather balloons begins.

1898

- The U.S. Weather Bureau establishes a hurricane warning network in the West Indies.

1901
- The Weather Bureau begins three-day forecasts for the Northeast.

1918
- The Weather Bureau begins issuing forecasts for military and air mail flights.

1919
- The American Meteorological Society, a network of meteorologists, is formed.

1922
- The radiosonde is invented. It allows monitoring of weather at high altitudes.

1935
- The first hurricane warning service begins.

Late 1930s
- Weather radar is developed.

1940
- The U.S. Weather Bureau is transferred to the Department of Commerce.

1941
- Two women are included in the U.S. Weather Bureau list of observers and forecasters.

1942
- The U.S. Navy gives the Weather Bureau 25 aircraft radars for meteorological use.

1944
- Due to WWII, the U.S. government begins hiring women as forecasters and observers for the U.S. Weather Bureau.

1950
- Numerical forecasts are made using computers.

1960
- The first weather satellite, TIROS I, is launched. It operates for 78 days.

1964
- The National Severe Storms Laboratory is established.

Timeline

1970

- The Environmental Science Services Administration (ESSA) becomes the National Oceanic and Atmospheric Administration (NOAA). The U.S. Weather Bureau becomes the National Weather Service.

1975

- The first Geostationary Operational Environmental Satellite (GOES) is launched into orbit. These are the first satellites able to track hurricanes.

1976

- Doppler radar for real-time operational forecasts and warnings is first used.

1993

- A blizzard deposits enough precipitation in one weekend to drastically change the water outlook for spring.

1997

- The nationwide Doppler (WSR-88D) radar network is fully deployed.

2005

- Hurricane Katrina strikes the Gulf Coast, resulting in the deaths of 1,833 people and becoming the most expensive natural disaster in U.S. history. The 2005 Atlantic hurricane season sets several records, including a record number of hurricanes.

2007

- The National Weather Service replaces the Fujita scale with the Enhanced Fujita scale to be more accurate with ranges of wind speeds.

2009

- The National Weather Service begins using the newest generation of supercomputers for weather prediction. These systems are able to make 69.7 trillion calculations per second.

2010

- NASA launches GOES-15 from Cape Canaveral, Florida, to join three other NOAA weather satellites in forecasting severe weather.

Ask & Answer

Introduction

- Why is meteorology an important career for women? What would science be like if only one race or gender worked in it?

Chapter 1

- Many early discoveries in meteorology were made by physicists. Physics is a branch of science that studies matter and energy. How is meteorology connected to other sciences?

- Why do you think so little information is available on early female scientists?

Chapter 2

- Kelly's communications background has been helpful in reaching her goal of becoming a successful broadcast meteorologist. Why are good oral and written communication skills important for broadcast meteorologists?

- Television isn't the only way that people get their weather forecasts and news. What are some other ways of getting this information? Could there be a difference in the accuracy of different channels of information? How could you tell?

- Television broadcast meteorologists often become local celebrities. Why do you think this happens? What makes viewers feel connected to their meteorologists?

Ask & Answer

Chapter 3

- Have you ever thought of math as a language? How do meteorologists use mathematics as a language to describe things that happen in the atmosphere?

- Have you ever been disappointed when you weren't chosen for something you really wanted to do? How did you handle it?

- Do you have a home or school emergency plan in case of a natural disaster? What are the main points of the plan? What is a good way to come up with a plan or improve the plan you have?

Chapter 4

- Have you ever entered a science fair? Science fairs are events where students gather to present the experiments they conducted. Sometimes, local scientists judge science fairs, so it's also a way to meet actual scientists!

- Pam felt a sense of community with the large group of females in her college meteorology program. How does this feeling of belonging to a group help when you're in school? Why is it helpful to know other female students studying the same subject as you?

- Have you ever taken on a leadership role, perhaps with a class project? What qualities do you think makes a good leader?

- Why is it important for women to be encouraged to go into STEM fields such as meteorology, fields that historically women have not been a large part of?

Glossary

accurate: in meteorology, the similarity of a forecast or calculation being close to actual measurements.

ad-libbing: speaking publicly without preparation.

aeronomy: the physics and chemistry of the upper atmosphere.

air mass: a large pocket of air that is different from the air around it.

air pressure: the weight of air that is pressing down on the earth.

algorithm: a step-by-step procedure for solving a complex problem.

almanac: a calendar with astronomical and weather-related data.

altitude: the height above the level of the sea. Also called elevation.

analyze: to study and examine.

astronomical: having to do with astronomy or the study of space.

astronomy: the study of stars, planets, and space.

atmosphere: the mixture of gases surrounding a planet.

atmospheric: having to do with the atmosphere.

augmented reality: a technology that superimposes a computer-generated image on a user's view of the real world.

barometer: an instrument that measures the pressure of the atmosphere.

cell: in meteorology, an air mass with powerful updrafts and downdrafts that can lead to severe weather.

circulation: the flow or motion of a fluid in or through a given area or volume.

climate: the average weather patterns in an area during a long period of time.

climate change: changes to the average weather patterns in an area during a long period of time.

climatology: the study of climate.

condensation: the changing of water vapor to liquid water, such as fog or dew.

convection: motions in a fluid that transport and mix the properties of the fluid, such as heat or moisture.

crops: plants grown for food and other uses.

current: the steady flow of water or air in one direction.

cyclical: occurring in cycles.

data: information in the form of facts and numbers.

de-ice: to remove ice from a surface.

density: the amount of matter in a given space, or mass divided by volume.

dew point: the temperature at which water starts to condense out of a particular air mass. The dew point indicates the moisture content of air.

dimension: a measurement.

dissertation: a long essay or paper written as a requirement of higher learning, particularly for PhD or doctorate programs.

diversity: variety; when referring to people, diversity means including individuals of varied race, gender, cultures.

dropwindsonde: a meteorological instrument dropped from an airplane. Also called a dropsonde.

dual-polarization radar: a radar tool that uses both horizontal and vertical radio waves to make accurate predictions of precipitation and weather.

electromagnetic: one of the fundamental forces of the universe, which is responsible for magnetic attraction and electrical charges.

electronic: describes a device that uses computer parts to control the flow of electricity.

equator: an imaginary line around the earth, halfway between the North and South Poles.

essence: the most important feature.

evolution: the process by which a species changes through generations due to mutation and natural selection.

export: to send goods to another country to sell.

FEMA: Federal Emergency Management Agency; a federal agency operating through the U.S. Department of Homeland Security during disasters.

forecast: to predict what will happen in the future.

frequency: in meteorology, the rate at which various weather phenomenon occurs.

front: a boundary between two different air masses that results in storms.

Fujita scale (also F-scale): a scale that measures the strength of tornadoes based upon wind speed.

gauge: an instrument or device for measuring.

geospatial: the relation to data associated with a specific location.

geostationary: a satellite moving in orbit over the equator, used by meteorological and communication satellites.

global: relating to the entire world.

global warming: an increase in the average temperature of the earth's atmosphere, enough to cause climate change.

goods: things to use or sell.

Hadley cell: a large-scale atmospheric convection cell in which air rises at the equator and sinks at medium latitudes, typically about 30 degrees north or south of the equator.

humidity: the amount of water vapor in the air.

hurricane: a severe tropical storm with winds greater than 74 miles per hour.

hygrometer: an instrument that measures humidity.

internship: a training period in service of an employer.

job shadowing: learning about a job by walking through the work day as a shadow to someone doing that job.

lake-effect snow: localized snow that forms on the downwind side of large lakes.

latitude: an imaginary line around the earth that runs parallel to the equator. It measures your position on the earth north or south of the equator.

matter: any material or substance that takes up space.

measure: to determine the size, amount, or degree of something by using an instrument or device marked in standard units.

mentor: an experienced and trusted advisor.

mesoscale: atmospheric phenomena having horizontal scales ranging from a few to several hundred miles, including thunderstorms, fronts, cyclones.

meteorologist: a scientist who studies and forecasts climate and weather.

meteorology: the study of weather.

microscale: a very small scale.

minority: a group of people that differs from the main group in race, gender, language, religion, or other differences. Minorities are often discriminated against.

monsoon: a seasonal wind that reverses direction between summer and winter and often brings heavy rains. Monsoons are most common in Asia, Mexico, and the southwestern United States.

natural disaster: a natural event, such as a fire or flood, that causes great damage.

Nor'easter: a powerful low-pressure system with coastal winds from the northeast that moves north along the Atlantic Coast.

observatory: a building with telescopes or other machines designed to observe objects in space.

Glossary

observe: to look at things carefully.

origin: the point where something begins.

ozone: a form of oxygen that heats the upper atmosphere by absorbing ultraviolet from sunlight.

pattern: something that happens over and over again.

phenomena: an observed event.

physics: a branch of science that studies matter and energy.

precipitation: any form of water that falls from clouds.

precursor: something that comes before another of the same kind.

predict: an estimate or guess of something happening in the future.

pressure: a force that pushes on something.

radar: a device that detects objects by bouncing radio waves off them and measuring how long it takes for the waves to return.

radiosonde: a small, lightweight box with weather instruments and a radio transmitter.

recruit: to get someone to join you or help you.

remote sensing: a method of obtaining information about an object without coming into physical contact with that object.

rotation: turning around a fixed point.

satellite: a manmade object placed into orbit around the earth, often carrying instruments to gather data.

scientific method: the way scientists ask questions and do experiments to try to prove their ideas.

scud: ragged, low clouds.

segregated: separated from the main group in society.

STEM: science, technology, engineering, and math fields.

stereotype: an overly simple picture or opinion of a person, group, or thing.

stratosphere: the layer of the earth's atmosphere above the troposphere, to about 31 miles above the earth.

storm surge: rising sea water or waves as a result of the winds and pressure of a storm.

supercell: a severe storm with nearly balanced updrafts and downdrafts that often produces hail and tornadoes.

synoptic: the use of meteorological data obtained simultaneously over a wide area for the purpose of presenting a comprehensive and nearly instantaneous picture of the state of the atmosphere.

Glossary

technology: tools, machinery, or equipment that increase scientific knowledge or develop from scientific knowledge.

theory: an unproven idea used to explain something.

topography: the natural features of the land, such as mountains.

trade wind: a wind that blows almost continually toward the equator from the northeast north of the equator and from the southeast south of the equator.

transformer: a devise used to reduce or increase the voltage of an alternating current.

tropical depression: a low-pressure disturbance that forms over warm tropical ocean waters and produces winds of 38 miles per hour or less.

tropical system: a low-pressure disturbance that forms over warm tropical ocean waters.

tropical wave: a long, north-south-oriented low-pressure system that moves from east to west across the tropics.

troposphere: the lowest part of the earth's atmosphere, where most of weather occurs.

vapor: a substance in a gaseous state.

variability: the ranges of a value.

velocity: the speed of something in a specific direction.

visibility: the distance that can be seen under weather conditions.

weather: what it's like outside—warm, cold, sunny, cloudy, rainy, snowy, or windy.

weather balloon: a balloon that carries instruments onto the atmosphere to collect data.

wind shear: a variation in wind speed and movement occurring at right angles to the wind's direction.

Resources

Books

- *DK Eyewitness Books: Weather.* Cosgrove, Brian. New York: DK Children, 2016.

- *National Geographic Kids Everything Weather: Facts, Photos, and Fun that Will Blow You Away.* Furgang, Kathy. Washington, D.C.: National Geographic Children's Books, 2012.

- *Extreme Weather: Weird Trivia & Unbelievable Facts to Test Your Knowledge About Storms, Climate, Meteorology & More (Challenge Yourself).* Probst, Jeff. New York: Puffin Books, 2017.

- *Meteorology: The Study of Weather (True Books: Earth Science),* Taylor-Butler, Christine. New York: Scholastic, 2012.

Websites and Museums

- NWS Education
  weather.gov/owlie

- GOES-R Mission Overview
  goes-r.gov/mission/mission.html

- Meteorology, National Geographic
  nationalgeographic.org/encyclopedia/meteorology

- Severe Weather 101, National Severe Storms Laboratory
  nssl.noaa.gov/education/svrwx101

- Weather, UCAR Center for Science Education
  scied.ucar.edu/weather

- Weather & Atmospheric Education Resources, NOAA
  www.noaa.gov/resource-collections/weather-atmosphere-education-resources

- WMO for Youth, World Meteorological Organization
  wmo.int/youth

Resources

Index